GW00371277

TRIAL FLIGHT GUIDE

TRIAL FLIGHT GUIDE

DAVID BRUFORD

Photography by Andrew Anderson
with the cooperation of Gwyn Aviation and
Airways Flight Training (Exeter) Ltd
Artwork by Jane Bruford

Technical Assistance
Chris Martin, Chief Flying Instructor
Exeter Flying Club, Devon

Airlife
England

Copyright © 1995 by David Bruford

The right of David John Bruford to be identified as the Author of this Work
has been asserted in accordance with the Copyright Designs and Patents Act 1988
Sections 77 and 78

First published in the UK in 1995
by Airlife Publishing Ltd

British Library Cataloguing in Publication Data
A catalogue record for this book
is available from the British Library

ISBN 1 85310 535 X

All rights reserved. No part of this book may be reproduced or
transmitted in any form or by any means, electronic or mechanical
including photocopying, recording or by any information storage
and retrieval system, without permission from the Publisher in writing.

Printed by Livesey Ltd., Shrewsbury

Airlife Publishing Ltd.

101 Longden Road, Shrewsbury SY3 9EB, England

Contents

Introduction

You may have received a trial lesson as a gift or decided to treat yourself as a taster to the possibility of taking up flying training. In either case, on the day of your flight you will be given a short lecture explaining what will happen, followed by around 30 minutes in the air.

To enjoy this short flight to the full it is useful to appreciate what is going on around you, both in the cockpit and outside. *The Trial Flight Guide* has been designed to help you learn the basics of flight and understand the instruments and controls in advance of the big day.

After a brief study of this book you should be able to sit in the pilot's seat, recognise most of the instruments, and appreciate what the controls do. This will leave you at ease to enjoy the pleasure and thrill of your first flight.

It is not necessary for you to learn every aspect covered in the book. After all, this is a pleasure flight. But do bear in mind you will be expected to take control of the aircraft, albeit under complete supervision, at some stage of your flight. The more you can learn beforehand the less you will have to pick up while you are in the air.

After your flight you may decide to take the experience further. Various options are open to you. You can take a few more lessons, building on the experience gained in your trial flight, you don't have to commit yourself to a full training course. You may even decide to go for a full private pilot's licence. The training involves around 45 hours of in-flight training plus time for ground lectures. The flying time from your trial flight can be used towards the licence. A full set of The *Air Pilot's Manuals* is available from Airlife Publishing or your flying club and will help you with the training required to obtain the licence.

If you decide to go further there's instrument and multi-engine ratings. A career path calls for a commercial or airline pilot's licence so who knows... every pilot started off with a trial flight.

An alternative is the Safety Pilot's Training Course. This has been designed for people who travel as a front seat passenger and want to be able to take over, fly and land the aircraft in the unlikely event of the pilot being incapacitated. The training involves around five hours flight and ten hours ground school. *The Safety Pilot's Training Manual*, also available from Airlife Publishing, gives full details and instructions for completing the course.

Happy Flying...

Certificate of Completion
Trial Flight

This is to certify that

_____

piloted the aircraft registered

_____

on

_____

Signed

_____

(Qualified Flying Instructor)

Stamp of Flight Organisation

TRIAL FLIGHT GUIDE

External aircraft view

The Theory of Flight

To keep an aircraft in the air a force is needed. This force is known as **lift**. It is produced by forcing a flow of air over an aerofoil section such as the wing and tailplane.

The wing and tailplane are built with a shape known as an aerofoil. An aerofoil is designed so that as it passes through the air the airflow over the top of the aerofoil has to travel a greater distance than the air travelling below. To travel this distance so that it reaches the back of the wing at the same time as the air below, it must speed up. Because of the increased speed, the air pressure is lower above the wing, than below. When enough airspeed, and consequently lift, is generated, the wing lifts into this low pressure area.

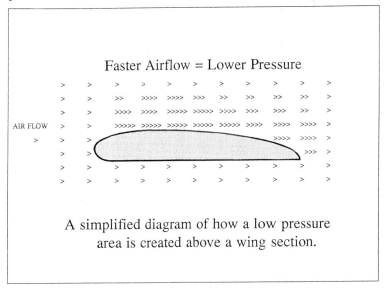

A simplified diagram of how a low pressure area is created above a wing section.

You might now consider that if that theory works then why not design a wing that has a much more curved upper surface. Unfortunately the airflow over a wing also has a negative side effect known as **drag**. An aircraft designer's job is to find a wing design that offers the highest lift and lowest drag. The aerofoil section must also be designed to point into the airflow at the most efficient angle, known as the **angle of attack**. If this angle is exceeded, for instance, by the aircraft being placed in too steep a climb, the airflow will break away from the upper wing surface, become turbulent, and cause the wing to stall.

To induce an aircraft to move through the air at a sufficient speed for the wing and tailplane to create lift a propeller is used. This is simply an aerofoil section that is spun through the air by the engine. A low pressure area is created in front of the curved surface of the propeller. This area of low pressure is so intense that it pulls the propeller and consequently the aircraft into it.

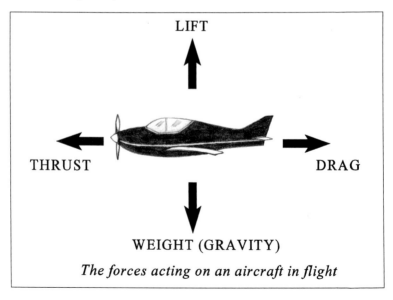

The forces acting on an aircraft in flight

THE THEORY OF FLIGHT

The propeller is always just behind this area, it can never catch up. With each revolution of the propeller moving forward more low pressure is being created just a little further ahead. The power generated by this action is known as **thrust**.

Thrust enables the aircraft to be pulled through the air at a sufficient speed for the wings to produce lift. The lift is more than enough to compensate for the weight of the aircraft and overcome the drag produced by the wings and fuselage. The balancing of these forces results in a very efficient flying machine.

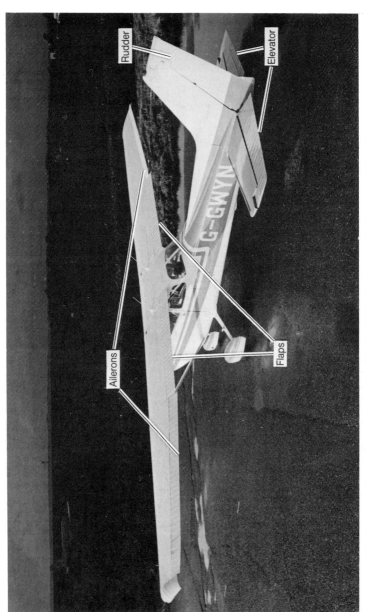

External View of the Aircraft Control Surfaces

Aircraft Controls and Control Surfaces

So with the basic theory out of the way let's look at how the aircraft is controlled. The picture opposite shows the various external surfaces of the aircraft used by the pilot. The picture below shows a cockpit view of the controls. The following sections explain the use and operation of each.

Cockpit View of the Control Column and Rudder Pedals

The Elevator or Stabilator

Some aircraft have a fixed tailplane to which a pivoted section is fitted. On others the whole tailplane pivots and

17

this is then known as a stabilator. In either case the moving section is used to change the amount of lift developed at the rear of the aircraft so that the nose of the aeroplane can be pointed up or down.

If the control column is pushed forward the elevator will move down and increase the tailplane's lift. This has the effect of pushing the nose of the aircraft down. If the control is pulled back, the lift is reduced and the tailplane will drop, resulting in the nose of the aircraft rising.

The Rudder

The rudder is operated by foot pedals. As with the control column the controls are duplicated on the pilot and passenger side. While on the ground these pedals are used to steer the aircraft and operate the brakes. For taxying, and in the air, the pedals are operated with your heels on the floor. This prevents accidental use of the brakes while landing or taking off. The brakes are operated by placing your whole foot on the pedal and pivoting the top forward. The use is very simple. Applying pressure to the right rudder pedal will turn the aircraft right. Using the right brake to slow the right wheel will result in a sharper turn. The left pedal turns the aircraft in the opposite direction.

In the air the rudder section at the rear of the fin is also operated by these pedals. If the right rudder pedal is depressed the panel will pivot out to the right, turning the aircraft in that direction. If the left rudder pedal is depressed the opposite will occur. The turning action is not very efficient and so in flight rudder movements are used as a complement to the ailerons. Technically the rudder is used to counteract **yaw**. This is an aviation term for a sideways skid.

AIRCRAFT CONTROLS AND CONTROL SURFACES

To avoid skidding turns the right rudder pedal is pressed when the control column is turned right and vice versa. How much rudder is needed is shown by a slip indicator. The use of this instrument is explained later in the book.

The Ailerons

All aircraft have a control column, either very similar to a car's steering wheel, or a stick. In either case the control movements are the same.

Turning the control column to the left will move the left aileron up and the right aileron down. This has the effect of increasing the lift on the right wing, making it rise, and reducing the lift from the left wing, making it fall. This results in the aircraft turning left. If the control column is turned right the reverse occurs.

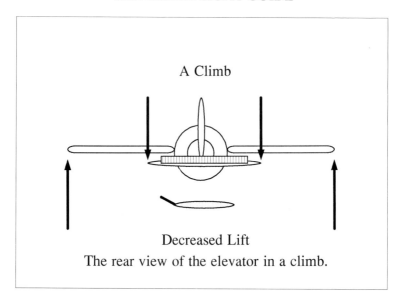

A Climb

Decreased Lift

The rear view of the elevator in a climb.

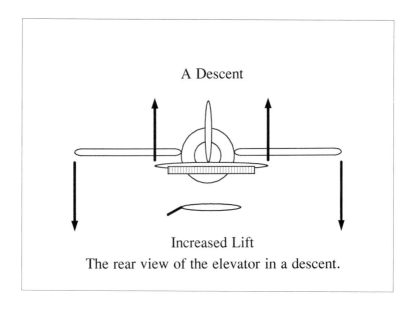

A Descent

Increased Lift

The rear view of the elevator in a descent.

AIRCRAFT CONTROLS AND CONTROL SURFACES

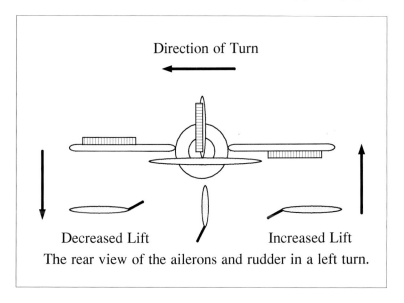

Direction of Turn

Decreased Lift   Increased Lift

The rear view of the ailerons and rudder in a left turn.

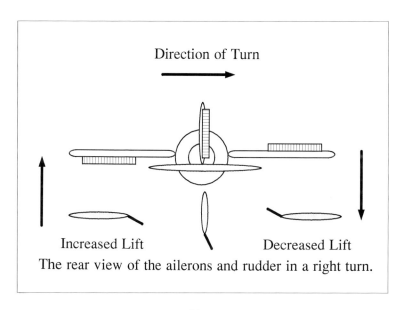

Direction of Turn

Increased Lift   Decreased Lift

The rear view of the ailerons and rudder in a right turn.

The Engine and Flight Controls

The Engine and Flight Controls

As you get into the aircraft on the day of your flight you will now know the position and use of the control column and rudder pedals. Let's now consider what some other knobs and dials are for.

The Throttle

This is a hand operated push/pull power control and works on the same basis as a car throttle. Pressing the control into the panel increases the power while pulling it outwards reduces it. As the power increases so does the thrust.

Any thrust in excess of cruise power, (that's the power setting that allows the aircraft to maintain a level height at its cruise speed), will be more than that required to overcome the weight and drag of the aircraft. As a result it will climb. Any setting lower than the cruise setting will allow the aircraft to descend. You might notice that after your flight the instructor will pull the throttle fully out as you approach to land. This will confirm to you that the aircraft will descend at a controlled speed if the power is reduced. It will also demonstrate that a modern light aircraft can glide for a safe landing in the event of engine failure.

Out of interest, if the knob is pulled out to its limit the engine will continue to run at a tick over speed, just like a car, it won't stop.

Carburettor Heat

The Carburettor heat knob is another push/pull control, similar to the throttle. When pulled out it operates a flap that channels hot air into the carburettor intake. This is a safety system as, due to the design of all carburettors, it is possible for ice to form from moist air and stick to the sides of the inlet. If left to build up it could block the air flow. To prevent icing the little knob is pulled out at regular intervals in conditions when carburettor icing could exist.

The Mixture Control

This is another push/pull control but coloured red to show its importance. If the control is pulled fully out, the fuel supply to the engine will be cut and the engine will stop.

It's used to lean the engine so that the carburettor gives the most efficient mixture of fuel and air for a given height. Air becomes thinner with altitude and the fuel to air mixture that makes the engine run at its best on the ground won't be the same as at, say, 3,000 feet. Motor cars don't suffer this problem as they rarely reach those heights!

The Trim Wheel

This is a little wheel, usually located between the two front seats. It's used to relieve the forward and backward pressure exerted by the pilot on the control column. In normal flight, often called **straight and level**, the trim wheel is adjusted so that the aircraft will fly happily level without any pilot participation.

THE ENGINE AND FLIGHT CONTROLS

The Flap Switch or Lever

Flaps are used to allow the aircraft to fly safely at slow speeds and are lowered as the aircraft approaches to land. Operating the flap switch or lever extends a panel of the wing, increasing its lift and consequently the drag. The drag increase isn't so important at this stage as flap is only used when the aircraft descends to land.

Control Panel

26

The Electronic Boxes

The Radio and Press to Transmit Switch

Aircraft radios vary in design but all have the same purpose. For safety reasons an aircraft is usually in contact with an air traffic control unit. Air traffic control, or ATC, will grant take off and landing clearances and can warn pilots if there are any other aircraft near them.

On your flight you will notice that before your aircraft moves from its parking place the instructor will ask for clearance from ATC. When you are ready for take off the instructor will advise ATC who will then grant a clearance to enter the runway.

Finally you will be given clearance to take off. After that, regular calls will be made just to let ATC know your height and the area you are flying in.

The press to transmit switch is usually located on the control column. Pressing the switch will let either front seat passenger talk to air traffic control through the headset microphone. It is designed only to transmit from the same side as the button that is being pressed, so don't worry if you are talking when the instructor is talking to ATC, they won't be able to hear you.

It is important for the instructor to be able to hear ATC messages and reply as required. To be able to do this and talk to you in between, a hand signal will be given asking you to be quiet for a moment.

Most aircraft also have a second, reserve radio for use in the unlikely event of the main radio failing. This is usually fitted below the main radio but won't be used at all during your flight.

Don't worry when the radio conversations start. It will be quick and contain some nonsensical sounding codes and information. If you decide to take up flying these will all be explained to you, but for this flight the instructor will talk to ATC in flying jargon and to you in plain English.

Typical Aircraft Radios

THE ELECTRONIC BOXES

The Headset and Headset Volume Control

When the engine is started and throughout your flight you will be expected to wear a headset. This is provided to dull the noise of the engine and to connect you to the radio and intercom. The intercom system enables the instructor to talk to you, and you to him or her. On most headsets there is a volume control knob. Use this before take off to adjust the volume to a level that allows you to hear the instructor and radio clearly.

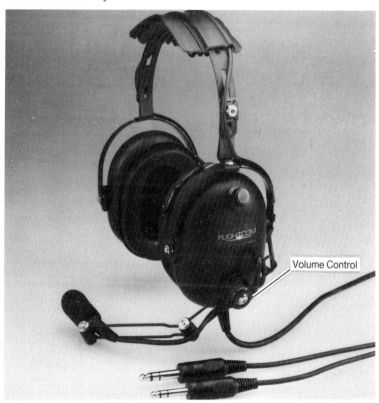

The Headset and Volume Control
(Photograph courtesy of R. D. Aviation Limited)

The Transponder

This device is fitted to most light aircraft and is a compulsory requirement for all airliners. The number selected and shown on the front of the transponder actually appears on a radar control screen. Each aircraft can be allocated a different number so that the position and call sign of each aircraft is known to the air traffic controller. On the radar screen the height of the aircraft is also shown and a little up or down arrow appears against it if the aeroplane climbs or descends.

All these factors help the controller make sure that you remain clear of any other aircraft in your area. The number displayed in the cockpit and appearing on the screen is called a **squawk**. When the aircraft is not under some form of radar control the number usually set on this display is 7000. Look out for that number and it will confirm that you are looking at a transponder. If the device is receiving a radar signal an orange light will flash at regular intervals confirming that someone on the ground knows exactly where you are.

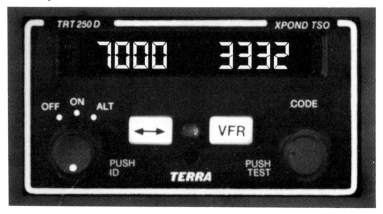

A typical Transponder
(Photograph courtesy of R. D. Aviation Limited)

THE ELECTRONIC BOXES

There will probably be some other electronic boxes fitted in the cockpit. Don't bother with them. They are used for radio navigation and probably won't even be switched on during your flight.

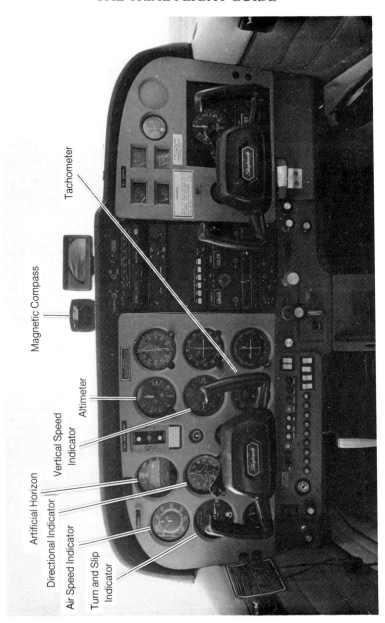

Tachometer

Magnetic Compass

Altimeter

Vertical Speed
Indicator

Artificial Horizon

Directional Indicator

Air Speed Indicator

Turn and Slip
Indicator

The Instruments

As it's impossible for even the most experienced pilot to accurately judge an aircraft's height, speed, or rate of descent, various dials are provided to give that exact information. As you first sit in the cockpit it will seem that there is a mass of dials. Viewed one by one they are very simple and only give simple information. Viewed in comparison with each other the instruments give the pilot a total picture of everything that is happening to the aircraft. Even when it's in cloud! Those dials not shown in the following section can be ignored.

The Artificial Horizon

THE INSTRUMENTS

The Artificial Horizon

This is known as the prime instrument and can replace the front view from the cockpit when the aircraft is in cloud or bad visibility. A miniature aircraft is shown on the centre of the display. In level flight the aircraft wings divide the upper blue area representing the sky from the black area that represents the earth.

This is used to display any turn, climb or descent that the aircraft makes very accurately, and without the pilot needing to look outside. The extent of the movement of the real aircraft is shown to exact scale by the miniature aircraft.

The Magnetic Compass

THE INSTRUMENTS

The Magnetic Compass and Directional Indicator

The magnetic compass is usually mounted on the top of the instrument panel or above it, this is to keep it as far away from magnetic fields as possible.

The compass will always, while in straight and level flight, point to magnetic north. Unfortunately because it's such a sensitive instrument it tends to swing around in climbs, descents and turns, making it hard to read.

To overcome these problems aircraft engineers invented the directional indicator which has a very stable directional compass display so this is used for all heading information. The magnetic compass is used to correct inaccuracies that slowly build up in the directional indicator.

The Directional Indicator

The Altimeter

THE INSTRUMENTS

The Height Indicator or Altimeter

The height indicator or altimeter is a very simple instrument which works on the same basis as a barometer that you may have in your home. It tells the pilot how high the aircraft is by constantly measuring the air pressure. Although this pressure varies from day to day it always reduces with height at the same rate. This reduction is measured and compared with the pressure over a known object and the result displayed on a dial.

Often this indication is compared with the air pressure at sea level as this is the basis of aeronautical charts. The dial has a small needle indicating thousands of feet and a longer needle showing hundreds. The illustration shows a height of 3,200 feet.

The Airspeed Indicator

THE INSTRUMENTS

The Air Speed Indicator

As we discussed in the earlier section for an aircraft to fly, lift must be generated by the wing. For enough lift to be generated an adequate airflow must be forced over the aerofoil section. The only way to tell that the aeroplane is travelling fast enough through the air is with an air speed indicator.

This instrument simply shows your speed through the air in a similar way that a car speedometer indicates your speed along the road. The instrument is colour coded to show various limits of speeds. In normal flight the indicated speed will always be in the green area.

At the speeds shown at the lower end of the white band the aircraft will stall. You will only see this speed register as the take off roll starts and as you slow down after landing. The upper limit of the green area shows the maximum speed of the aircraft.

The Vertical Speed Indicator

THE INSTRUMENTS

The Vertical Speed Indicator

The vertical speed indicator is used to limit the rate of climb or descent.

This is shown in relation to a full minute at that rate. For instance, if the indicator is showing a climb rate of 500 feet per minute and that climb is kept steady for 30 seconds you will climb 250 feet.

If you experience a few bumps or drops in your flight this instrument will waver up and down around the 0 point. The illustration shows a descent rate of 500 feet per minute.

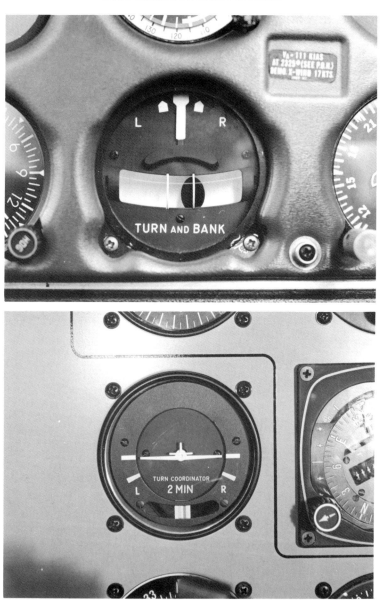

Typical Examples of Turn & Slip or Turn & Bank Indicators

THE INSTRUMENTS

The Turn and Slip Indicator

This instrument is also known as a turn and bank indicator. It is very similar to the artificial horizon and it's actually used as a safety back up for that instrument. The only difference is that it can't show a climb or descent. The slip indicator is at the bottom of the display. It is simply a curved glass tube with a weighted ball in the bottom. The ball responds to gravity and will normally be between two 'in limits' lines. While turning, the ball will be thrown outwards by centrifugal force showing that the aircraft is yawing or skidding into a turn.

Pressing the rudder pedal in the same direction as the turn will make the ball move back to the centre, confirming that the turn is balanced.

The Tachometer

THE INSTRUMENTS

The Tachometer or Revolutions per Minute Indicator

An instrument again similar to that in a car. In a car or aircraft it is usually called a rev counter. With a car it is used to show when a gear change would be most efficient. As an aircraft doesn't have gears its use is far simpler.

The green coloured section shows the engine speed for cruising or level flight. A red line at the upper limit of this section indicates the limit of the speed that the engine should operate at. In a climb or cruise the engine is designed so that it can't easily over-rev but in a descent it could happen. To prevent this the throttle setting is reduced. If you notice the rev counter as you come in to land you will see that it is well below the green area. This shows that the engine is just ticking over.

There are also several other dials in the cockpit, don't let them concern you. They are used for radio navigation and probably won't even be switched on during your flight. All the interesting instruments have been covered in the previous text and will be the only ones used by the instructor during your flight.

The Day of the Flight

You will have probably booked the slot for your trial flight several days or even weeks ahead. On the morning of the flight take a look at the weather.

If it seems anything other than a sunny, cloud free day then give the flying club a ring. They will tell you if the weather is suitable or if the flight should be postponed and re-booked for another day.

Good flying weather is not always the same as good weather for people on the ground, so a quick phone call may save you an unnecessary journey.

Dress bearing in mind that the temperature does get a little cooler with height, and although most light aircraft have heaters, they are not always used. If you are cold in the aircraft don't hesitate to tell the instructor.

Equip yourself for a short walk across the grass to the aeroplane. Airfields are, out of necessity, on large flat areas, so the wind can be quite penetrating on a cold day.

An essential item for the flight is a pair of sun glasses. Even on a cloudy day your flight might be made above the cloud and although some light aircraft have sun visors they are not known for their effectiveness.

At the Airfield

When you arrive at the flying club present yourself at reception. They will introduce you to your flight instructor and he or she will take you off to a quiet area for what is known as a ground briefing.

The briefing, as with the flight, will include all or just some of the following sections. The amount of detail and actual flying will depend on the amount of time available. In the briefing, you and the instructor will be able to have an informal chat about the flight. Having read this book you will, of course, be familiar with the basic principles of flight and the way that the controls affect the aircraft. However, a verbal explanation, probably with the aid of a model aircraft, should clarify any doubtful points.

Take this opportunity to ask about any aspect of flying that you don't understand or that particularly interests you.

If you want to fly over an area you know well, now is the time to ask if it is possible. It isn't always feasible as there are various airspace restrictions here and there, but if it can be done, the instructor will be sure to oblige.

The Pre-Flight Checks

When it is time to board the aircraft you will sit in the left-hand seat. This is the principal seat as most of the instruments are placed for a clear view from that position. The reason for this is that most aircraft are of American design. As American cars drive on the wrong side of the road it is logical that they should design their aircraft so that the pilot sits on the same side as a car driver.

All training aircraft have dual controls for the control column, rudder and brake pedals. The throttle, carburettor and mixture controls are placed in the middle for easy access for both pilots. The instructor will demonstrate the movement of the control column and show you how the surfaces move.

After this demonstration, and with the instructor's assistance, you should adjust the seat so that you can reach the top of the rudder pedals with your feet. The control column should also be at a comfortable distance. The instructor will also help you in doing up the seat belt which should be tight but not restrictive. An explanation will also be given on how to operate the seat, seat belt and door to exit the aircraft in the unlikely event of an emergency or precautionary landing away from the airfield.

When you are comfortable the instructor will carry out the normal external pre-flight checks of the aircraft before joining you in the cabin.

The final fitting is the headset. Most types are adjustable so juggle it around until you are comfortable. The microphone should be as close as possible to your mouth without actually touching it. One tip. If you are wearing glasses put these on before the headset. If you try it the other way around it can be quite painful!

Up, Up and Away

The instructor will run through various checks before and after starting the engine. A clearance must be granted by air traffic control before the aircraft may be taxied to a holding point just off the main runway.

To ensure that you are not talking when a radio call is being made or received the instructor will suggest a hand signal that he or she will use. When this is given just stop talking. You, or the instructor might be in mid-sentence when the signal is given. Don't be offended. It's essential for these conversations to take place and your conversation can continue when the call has been completed.

The trip from the parking place to the holding point will be your first opportunity to steer the aircraft. This is achieved by pushing the foot operated rudder pedals right or left. When the pedals are pressed at the top they will pivot forward operating the individual wheel brakes. The instructor will remain in full control but will allow you to get the feel of the steering.

At the holding point further engine and control checks are completed. One of these involves checking the engine function at high power and at tick-over and is a compulsory requirement. The instructor may talk through some of these checks with you, explaining why they are being carried out.

After being granted a further clearance the aircraft will be lined up with the runway. At this stage ensure that your heels are on the floor and just resting on the rudder pedals. This is to prevent inadvertently operating the brakes while on the take-off roll. The instructor will suggest that you lightly hold the control column with your left hand and feel the movements being made.

Full power will then be applied. After a short take-off roll the air speed indicator will reach the speed at which the aircraft will create enough lift to fly, you will feel the control column being pulled slightly back and ... you're in the air.

In Flight Instruction

While making the initial climb the instructor will point out that the altimeter is showing an increasing height, the vertical speed indicator is showing a climb and that the airspeed indicator is at a steady speed.

At around 500 feet the aircraft will be turned towards your chosen flight area and a climb continued to a height that the instructor considers best for good visibility. This part of the flight offers a good opportunity for each instrument's function to be explained. As before, if there is anything you don't understand, just ask.

After the aircraft has been settled down in a straight and level flight the instructor will offer you control of the aircraft. All control movements will be closely monitored so don't worry about losing control.

The only instruments that should concern you at this stage are the air speed indicator and altimeter but even these only require an occasional glance. Don't get fixed on the instruments, there's a great view outside!

To keep the aircraft in straight and level flight the view of the horizon is used. The instructor will pick a ground reference point or even a cloud and ask you to fly towards it. Any movements of the control column should be very gentle and preferably with just one hand. Slight left or right and forward or backward movements will steer you at a steady level and in a straight line.

Although your main aiming point will be outside the cockpit your instructor may also point out the directional indicator. This will, providing you are flying straight, show a steady heading.

Once you're happy with straight and level, the instructor will ask you to turn the aircraft, probably with a demonstration first. Turning is achieved by moving the control column in the direction of the turn. This is complemented by rudder pressure on the same side as the turn, but only enough to keep the ball in the centre of the slip indicator. The nose of the aircraft will tend to drop slightly so a little back pressure on the control column will be required.

As soon as the wings are banked to the required angle the control column is moved back to roughly the central position. The turn will continue with just a little right or left adjustment of the control being required.

To return to straight and level the control column is turned in the opposite direction to the turn until the wings are level. The nose will tend to rise. To correct this, the slight back pressure may be released.

A climb and descent may also be demonstrated. This is a simple procedure that starts from straight and level flight. Pulling the control column lightly back will cause the nose of the aircraft to rise. This will cause the indicated air speed to reduce and so a higher throttle setting may be required for a prolonged climb.

At the top of the climb the control column is pushed slightly forward to regain the normal horizon view and the throttle reset to the cruise setting. A descent is achieved by a gentle forward pressure on the control column. This will cause the airspeed to increase and so the throttle setting may be reduced to maintain the cruise speed on the rev counter.

To stop the descent the control column is pulled back to regain the normal horizon view and the throttle reset to the cruise setting.

If time permits it may also be possible for the instructor to show how the wind affects an aircraft in flight. While cruising in straight and level flight the air speed indicator will always show the same speed through the air but the speed over the ground may alter considerably.

A hot air balloon will travel along with the air in which it flies. An aircraft has an engine that gives it the ability to travel in any direction the pilot wishes, but it is still affected by the wind.

If for instance an aircraft cruises at 80 knots directly into a 10 knot wind its speed over the ground will only be 70 knots. If the wind is directly behind it the speed over the ground would be 90 knots.

Wind speed calculations are therefore very important to an aircraft especially when working out the time required for a trip. Such estimates are calculated on the ground speed and as flights are rarely made directly into or with the wind, a cross wind calculation is required.

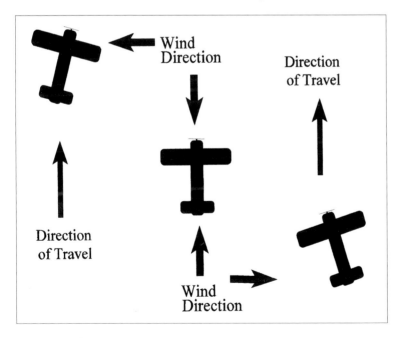

THE TRIAL FLIGHT GUIDE

If an aircraft flies with a cross wind, which is a wind at any other angle than directly in front or behind, the nose of the aircraft must be turned slightly into the wind to enable a straight course to be maintained.

This angle is particularly noticeable if there is a cross wind on the final approach to land. Although the instructor may be pointing the nose of the aircraft away from the runway centre line the aircraft will still be flying in line with it.

Unfortunately, and probably just as you are really starting to enjoy the fun of flying, it will be time to return to the airfield. Again the instructor will ask you to follow the control movements as the aircraft descends, lines up with the runway, and lands. As the aircraft leaves the runway you may have another opportunity to taxi towards the parking area.

The time between the engine being shut down and the walk back to the club house will be your final opportunity to ask any questions. Don't forget to have your certificate signed and stamped by the instructor. Even if you decide not to take any further flights you will have a permanent memento of the occasion.

Enjoy your flight.

Quick Reference Glossary

Aerofoil	A shaped section with a curved upper surface in the design of a wing or tailplane.
Aileron	A movable section fitted to the rear of a wing which may be pivoted up or down to increase or decrease the lift of one side of the wing resulting in a turn.
Altimeter	The instrument used to show an aircraft's height above a known object, for instance, the sea or an airfield.
Angle of Attack	The angle between the wing and the airflow.
Artificial Horizon	The main reference instrument used to control an aircraft while in cloud.
ATC	Air traffic control.
Carburettor Heat	A device used to divert hot air through the carburettor air intake and prevent an ice build up.
Clearance	Permission issued by air traffic control for an aircraft to taxi, take off or land.
Cruise	Level flight with the engine set up for maximum fuel economy.
Drag	A negative force produced by an aircraft as it passes through the air.

Elevator	A movable section fitted to the rear of the tailplane that may be pivoted to increase or decrease the lift resulting in a climb or descent.
Flaps	A section attached to the inside rear of a wing that can be lowered to reduce the stalling speed on an approach to land.
Holding Point	A point just off the main runway where a pilot may perform the pre-take off checks.
Intercom	A closed circuit radio system enabling aircraft crew or passengers to talk to each other.
Lift	The force produced by a flow of air passing over an aerofoil.
Mixture Control	A device used to adjust the fuel/air mixture to the carburettor for maximum fuel efficiency.
Radio Navigation	A method of navigating by using ground based radio beacons.
Rudder	A movable section fitted to the rear of the fin that can be pivoted to turn the aircraft left or right and prevent yaw.
Squawk	A number on the transponder, selected by the pilot and displayed on a radar controller's screen.
Stall	The condition where an aerofoil section ceases to create lift due to an excessive angle of attack or low airspeed.
Tachometer	A display used to show the revolutions per minute at which the propeller is turning.

QUICK REFERENCE GLOSSARY

Taxi	Any movement of an aircraft on the ground.
Throttle	The device used to increase or decrease the fuel flow to the engine, resulting in an increase or decrease in thrust.
Tick-over	A throttle setting where the engine is producing the minimum power possible without stopping.
Transponder	A device fitted to the aircraft that sends height, identification and location information to a ground based radar screen.
Trim Wheel	A system used to relieve any forward or back pressure on the control column allowing the aircraft to fly level without any pilot input.
Thrust	The force created by the aerofoil section of a propeller.
Turn & Slip Indicator	The turn element of the display shows the amount that the aircraft's wings are banked. The slip indicator shows the amount of yaw.
Vertical Speed Indicator	A display that shows the rate of climb or descent of the aircraft.
Yaw	The effect of an aircraft skidding sideways.

Index

THE TRIAL FLIGHT GUIDE